# How to Pour Madness into a Teacup

## Abegail Morley

Published by Cinnamon Press
Meirion House
Glan yr afon
Tanygrisiau
Blaenau Ffestiniog
Gwynedd
LL41 3SU
www.cinnamonpress.com

The right of Abegail Morley to be identified as author of this work has been asserted by her in accordance with the Copyright, Designs and Patent Act, 1988. Copyright © 2009 Abegail Morley
ISBN: 978-1-907090-00-4
British Library Cataloguing in Publication Data. A CIP record for this book can be obtained from the British Library.

Designed and typeset in Palatino by Cinnamon Press. Cover design by Mike Fortune-Wood from original artwork 'Face in Stone' by Madartists, © agency Dreamstime

Printed in Great Britain by the MPG Books Group, Bodmin and King's Lynn

Cinnamon Press is represented in the UK by Inpress Ltd www.inpressbooks.co.uk and in Wales by the Welsh Books Council www.cllc.org.uk.

# Acknowledgements

I would like to thank Bill Greenwell and all at Poetic Biscuits
for their help with this collection.

Some of the poems included here have been published,
sometimes in different versions, in *Anon*, *Dream Catcher*,
*Envoi*, *Iota*, *Inside Out*, *Interpreter's House*, *Orbis*, *Other Poetry*,
*Poetry Express*, *Pulsar*, *Rain Dog*, *South*, *The New Writer* and
*The Spectator*.

'Counsellor', 'Her Likeness', 'Therapy' and 'Memory Game'
all appear in the anthology *The Sandhopper Lover* (Cinnamon
Press, 2009) and the title poem, 'How to Pour Madness into
a Teacup' won the *Orbis* Readers' Award in 2008.

# Contents

Madness

# How to Pour Madness into a Teacup

# Schedule

She dances through
the middle of days,
blends memories with oil of lavender, keeps
conversations in scrapbooks.

She papers the walls with anecdotes,
pinches her lips to hoard her thoughts,
and when asked for her opinions
plucks on her mouth like a harpist
playing on gut strings.

# Counsellor

The shine of his hair
swept back by his hand

startles her. He leaves
with her words recorded

in his red *This is Your Life* folder
tucked under his arm.

He goes before she has finished,
so she swallows her words

and the unspoken sentence
slips down her throat.

# Yellow Trousers

She can talk forever.
He does not have that long,
there are people,
appointments.
They are not her business.

He wears yellow: odd,
he has not worn it before.
It does not suit him.
He is not quite there:
his head is outside

with his yellow trousers
in the park perhaps,
or a coffee shop.
His sleeves rub the table,
dirty at the cuff.

# Word Play

She looks at her words hanging up like washing.
She thought she was told to hang
them for medical reasons, but realises
she was told to think before she speaks—
not to air her dirty washing in public.

She writes in felt-tip pen across the walls,
big, annotated letters, huge doodles,
endless illustrations to bulk out her words:
to make it look as if she has more to say.

# From Her VCR Manual

Picture this… it started during the play

[cue… she searches for the beginning]
after 15 seconds he starts:

[cue… move forward, quickly, easily]
during the 46 minutes he performed
he has been special.

[cue… stand-by position]
he longs for it,
he wants to be desired,
he must be desired.

[cue… in a forward direction]
every time he performed
he was high,
he pushed forward, fast,
marked seconds, minutes.

[cue… play at speed]
he plays, he displays
time after time
he wants,
must have,
want
have.

[cue… switch to the beginning]
after 15 seconds he starts:
he longs to play,
he wants to play,
when he finds what he wants
it is finished.

# Nighthawks

His hand near hers
steals her breath,
wraps her between his lips
replaces her words with his.

His hand refuses to touch hers.
She is safe if she doesn't look up.
She will not break his thoughts.

His hand near hers but not touching
might light another cigarette
and give her some more time.

His loveless face removes her
and he goes into the green street
to mend his life in the arms of another.

# Waiting Room

She smells vanilla in the air,
hears his half-baked truth

and holding out her emptiness
is surprised how much
space it takes.

She moves the chairs, puts them in order
sequenced by colour, lilac on one side,
red on the other.

Folding the room around her,
she tucks in its edges and is
swallowed whole.

# Cognitive Behaviour Therapy

She snaps her limbs shut,
sits in the chair,
her hands on her knees
extremities wound so tightly
breath might firecracker her body.

She is installation art
a work in progress
defined by her puppetry.
He tells of a new world.
She sees it before her.

He leaves, and her unforgotten past
cuts her edges.
A scissored paper-chain of a woman
extends across the room.

# Charity Case

The illness is so efficient
there are no loose ends.
There are no ends at all.

She cannot tie the illness up,
leave it in a spectacular loop
and give it to a friend.

It follows her in Crimplene,
it could not choose silk or satin
and so she is
haunted by viscose.

# Exaggerations

She looks down at guilty ankles,
and cannot lift her head.

He tells her mania is harmful,
but she doesn't think

that's the type she has.
Hers is being the sun at midnight.

# Beating Time

Smooth sheets wrap, unwashed,
around her body; she is
bruised by the dark.

Familiar night-sweats
soak her skin:
they are shadowy, damp.

Chesting the pillow,
resting her chin,
she re-starts her count,
avoiding odd numbers.

# Photo Album

She flips the pages too fast
a corner of his face

breaks away between her fingers.
She feels his brisk, brittle exterior,

the squeak of his shoes,
her grandmother's voice:

*It's a sign he hasn't paid for them.*
His tight expression.

She wants to grow into his features,
his face against hers
when the album is shut,

but skin lifts from her face,
tightens around the cheek bones,
fearing what she might say.

# Slice

Between biting his burger
and talking to her,
he stops at the kerb
of Gerald Street.

He smiles at her,
squeezes tomato pips
between his teeth,
slides them through gaps,
and licks them away without a thought.

# No School for Madness

Plucking her vision out of the air
straightening it,
she pours it in poster paint—

with perfect, cupid bows
from thigh to toes,
a felt-tip frenzy.

The untidiness of it all.
Painted legs and arms
escape the folds of her body.

Pulling herself out of its hold,
shaking it around her
she steps out of its circle
and closes the door behind her.

# Wednesday with the Psychiatrist

The first day they met
she ticked all the boxes
in his questionnaire
and stole his pen.

She sat in the waiting room
at the children's table,

tiny chairs, crayons, blank paper,
where she could draw a purple giraffe
with as many legs as she wanted
and not be medicated.

# Out of Reach

He lets her slip forward
into someone else's hands,

shrugs her off on Sundays
outside The Lemon Grove.

His arms discuss her life—
wide gestures stretch the air.

He divides her in two:
the before, the after.

She sees his nails
for the first time: cut, clean.

# Closing In

She cries on the phone—
Tube humming in the background,

occasionally she is told to
*mind the gap.*

The space between their lives is
widening into a stretched yawn

and the day, cutting itself in half,
gives an upwards embrace.

# Waterlogged

He builds a bridge and a raft.
The bridge doesn't reach the other side

and the raft keeps taking in water.
She loves him, but that is not enough:

he leaves her
treading water until she

dives deep, swims
in slow motion, and beneath

the surface watches
the ripples on his face.

# Bridge

Running high up into herself
she takes off from the bridge
where they met, running their hands
over soft moss.

Stepping off is easy,
like running too fast as a child,
moon rapidly calling in night
before she is ready.

# Therapy

Unwinding her legs from
the chair that holds them

she dives underwater,
her screams softening.

She lives in a world of action replays.

# Submerging

Caught in the water's throat,
her lips cling like limpets
to her drowning mouth.
Her face swells,
it purls and falls.

Her cries stream upwards,
bubbles spume on the surface.

# Late

Her hands lay flat on paper
laid out as if by a mortician,

polished and preserved.
Her youth is written, recorded,

blue-veined ink lapping
the shoreline of her pages.

Only drowning can save her.

# Edge

She gnaws a flap of skin
on her thumb
prises it off and leaves it
to the elements,
hooked as a fish
between her fingers,
netted, gutted,
served up at his table.

# One Last Time

His head is merely breaths away.
She waits for him, for formality.
She's spent too much on sentiment.

She wants to use his life, to write down his spine.

It's summer now. The sun
speaks in long shadows.

He reads her by her scars.
Does he remember writing them?

# Shopping List

She walks arm in arm with lilies,
grabs at items on the aisle—
coffee, biscuits, beans.

Raw flesh drips
from her fingertips
over the oranges.

He imagines a home,
a table by the window,
flowers in a vase.

# Low Season

### i

Arcades and burger bars—
a shanty town in the winter wind
lies empty in expectation
of summer suns.

Wall's ice cream flags
thrash on poles
promising a sun-baked future.

Coffee on the dashboard steams
up the window. He draws a
smiley face which she rubs out
reaching for a biscuit.

### ii

Sunday, posed
snapshot, last shot,
hand out of focus
as if she knew she was leaving.

# They Could Always Sit Somewhere Else

They survive on their own paths,
bits of their lives
in the seams of their pockets,

a jumble of tobacco, sweet wrappers
and a thick stickiness
they cannot explain.

There's a crumble of biscuit
damp and unforgiving
under her fingernails.

A fragment of paper,
a list, a receipt,
rolled into a ball.

She pulls out her hand,
ball between finger and thumb
and launches it into the air.

It falls in the waste of verge
and perhaps that is the point,
that there never was a point.

# Justice

She won't let a blink disturb her
and stares as he strips her judgement,
holds it up like washing
announces its dirt.

His lips, conspirators,
sticking together,
neither giving up the other.

Earlier, they sat in the pew,
cold visitors, unholy.

# Laundry

She says, with a smile
that belongs to someone else,
that what she prefers
are red knickers.

She puts them on spin
with her whites
and watches the redness
drip down the glass.

# Moving On

He removes the picture
he'd hung with a sweep of masculinity.

She watches its sharp edges, straight lines,
how empty it is, how much of a box.
The thin brass nail is bent.

She thinks of strong foundations,
a Bible verse she can't quite remember

and wonders (for a split second)
if stronger nails might have saved them.

# Now He has Left

She stashes the tears under her pillow.
They gasp for air.

She presses, keeps pressing down
until the only movement
is the tremor of her hands,
the pulsing in her neck.

By day she stuffs them in her purse as
loose change—
turns heads, then tails
over and over,
metallic. Her tongue

is pressed between grave clothes.
She feels his pillow,
puts grief beneath it. In the morning
she clears his name from her throat.

# How to Pour Madness into a Teacup

She hangs her tears at the front of the house
cuts the rain in half and puts time
in the hot black kettle. She sits in the kitchen
reading the teacup full of small dark tears;

it's foretold the man in the wood
hovers in the dark rain above the winding path.
The man is talking to her in moons,
she is laughing to hide her tears

and with little time, she secretly
plants the moons in the dark brown bed.
She shivers, thinks the man is watching
as the jokes of the child dance

on the roof of the house. Tidying,
she carefully puts hot rain in the teacup,
sings as she hangs her tears on a string
and watching the dance, thinks herself mad.

# Cry Baby

As soon as nobody is looking
she will sew the tears

to the hem of her coat
with thread that doesn't match

so she can watch their wounds
bleed along the stitching.

She will sew them in pairs
so they can hold hands.

# Imprint

She leaves a handprint on her cheek.
Finger shapes form in flesh
as she wipes tears across her face,

drags them along bone,
so tightly the skin skims the jaw.

He watches her contortions,
smooths down her spine,
ties her arms behind her back
to keep them out of harm's way.

# Holding Out

He takes her hands.
She wants to peel them apart

as if they were oranges
released from their rind,
white veins pulling away from skin
in stinging citrus curls.

## Breathing Lessons

The room, opening out its gaze,
undresses her, peels skin to bone.
The arch of her throat and the white
slice of shoulder are not to be trusted.

Sculpting her ribcage, polished smooth
beneath its touch, hands follow
the dip of bone, trace from back to front,
widening her ribs

until she catches her breath.

# A Consultation

She tries not to inhale,
she has made that mistake before.

Breathing through the mouth
is asking for trouble.

Her chair is damp, discoloured.
She must remember not to touch her face

until she washes her hands.

She worries how to leave the room
without touching the handle.

# Exhale

She bites her bottom lip, draws blood.
Her hand hides her mouth—

the burden of his lips still hangs on hers

and as he leans in,
the smell of his hair meets hers,
his odour leaving itself on her sleeve,
burrowing between the stitches.

Their only connection is exhalation:
her breath snagged,
she hears only his breathing.

# Hanging On

She will straighten him out,
string him the full length

of her sitting room
with green garden twine,

and see the sun's glare
stretching across his face,

his words, false idols
glistening in his mouth.

# Empty

He washes his hands.
He washes his hands.
He washes his hands on her,
over and over.

He traces her hand with his finger
around the wrist
and pulling back her hair,
ties it in a tight, neat, ponytail
letting it hang

in a line of blonde
that touches her T-shirt.

# Touched

She won't touch the arms of the chair:
they have soaked up twenty years of madness,
they are steeped in it.
He is the serious, silent listener
stern as a constant funeral.

Always cover the dead, they can still express how they feel;
lies on the other hand should be kept uncovered.
She sometimes catches the truth but usually drops it.
Tonight she will have to wash the madness out of her jeans.

# Misplaced

She snatches a letter, a word,
and harvests her head,
finding the middle of a sentence.

She writes it on her palm
with her index finger
and flattens her hand on the glass.

He watches as she leaves her mark
in cheap breath on his window.

# Up His Sleeve

Her mouth congeals.
She wipes words upwards
across her cheek.

At the hairline
they snap their edges.
They break around her jaw.

He stiffens his eyes
deals his anger,
a five-card draw.

# Her Turn

Smearing her reflection down the mirror,
she observes herself pressing the lift button
with her knuckle so she doesn't leave prints.


She gives a sideways glance at the receptionist,
her razor lips scratching the glass.

She sits, and watches them
as they slip into their seats
like syrup down a child's throat.

At intervals their names are called, and they go
sucking out air as they leave.

She knows what they say, and stays
winding their stories round her fingers
and, knotting them at both ends
plays cat's cradle with their conversations.

# Caged

His fat fingers
clutch feathers.

Through narrow bars
he listens for air
between her clipped wings,

scratches the lock,
his hands desperate to reach her.

She hardly lifts her head.
The floor of the cage
dusted with words.

# Aviarist

She hears him on the stairwell,
and folds herself tightly as if wings
concertina'd at her side.

He rakes them down.
She is mute with dimming eyes
and a beak poked in blood.

He drags his hands down her sides,
hardly a scratch of light shows
between his elbow and her body.

His watch creeps, unblinking, along her skin.

# Deliverance

The tether of the passion
strangles her:
at the moment where they met,
she sits, an empty promise in the dark.

Under her tongue
she holds a caged bird's squeal.
Her mouth is thick with feathers.

# Hiding Place

She wipes mud and blood
down the front of her dress

her calves ache with crouching
her heart urgent

hands ready by her side.

# 4am

She scrapes back her hair
        a tight knot
   nothing must come between
her and the wall
       scrub with bleach
attack
        each
           stain


scalded frantic hands
       gloveless
10 inch J-cloth
    wipes
eyes blister
      hands read
        Braille dirt


hands on cloth
            in bucket
white wash
      wash white
    wall wash
      white wall

# Graffiti

She has spent the last three nights
scrubbing with bleach,
yet still the paintwork howls,
keeping her awake.

It's 4am, she follows the grain
with red cracked fingers
tracing a sentence.

But there are too many words
and some break free.
She put candles around them.

She watched them last night.
She did not retreat
but sat amongst them
guarding them from him.

# Memory Game

The toes of her socks are bleached,
her fingers red and cracked, her knuckles sore,
strands of fringe, white as an old woman's.

He can see at her noon appointment
how she spent last night in manic splendour,
the day lost, the memory gone.

The only evidence is at home:
clean walls, the smell of swimming pools.

# Night Watch

i

She pulls down her sleeves,
hides behind burnt eyes
and lines of charcoal.

*Forgive me*, rolls like a marble
on his tongue.

She speaks his name,
leaves it on the tip of her tongue
too long—he walks
beyond the railings,
shadows clipping his heels.


ii

After forgiveness
a cold ache echoes down corridors.
She holds out her hand,
but doubts it will be filled tonight.

Blue from the night
she bends away from his hands,

and in the blackness
binds the edges of her body

to streamers of yellow light,
and weeps at its weaving.

# Turn Tail

The sofa is
plumped up with goodbyes.

It releases a feather
a whitetail feather
a gamecock's feather.

She and the feather
contemplate his departure,
one of them calling him back.

# Appropriate Measures

She roughs out his life with a chisel,
chips away
in straight, accurate lines.
Her touch is cold on cold.

She carves his frame,
scrapes his shape.
Fine flakes collect
beneath her nails.

She wipes her hand on her jeans:
a line of red powder down her thighs.

# Packing

## i

She bends backwards
further than the chisel needs
hammers hard
and a line extends across his chest
cracking apart his heart.

Dust lines her sticky lungs.

He litters the floor with his jumble of limbs—

now and then she unearths a wink, a cheek,
a frightened lip.

## ii

She puts his limbs in the suitcase
lets it lean against her ankles
as she zips up the contents.

She picks him out of her jumper:
an eyelash, a pimple,
a flake from the shaver.

She can smell him on her cuffs.

## Passenger

She packs her past in a red suitcase,
out of style, gaudy:
*Look at me*, it shouts,
a merchant of insanity.

It circles the terminus
round and round on the conveyor belt
like some terminal illness
waiting to begin.

She didn't move fast enough,
lost herself to its motion
and the inconsolable past,
unresolved, moves on too.